An Evensong

An Evensong

Poems

Nathaniel A. Schmidt

Foreword by Ethan Lewis

RESOURCE *Publications* · Eugene, Oregon

AN EVENSONG
Poems

Resource Publications
An Imprint of Wipf and Stock Publishers
199 W. 8th Ave., Suite 3
Eugene, OR 97401

www.wipfandstock.com

PAPERBACK ISBN: 978-1-5326-0481-2
HARDCOVER ISBN: 978-1-5326-0483-6
EBOOK ISBN: 978-1-5326-0482-9

Manufactured in the U.S.A.

For my parents:

who love the verse of God in me
more than my verses about God

Soli Deo Gloria

"Art is the signature of man"

—*G.K. Chesterton*

Contents

CONTENTS

Foreword

Channel how our world you wish to change alters
so you might proclaim your aria, sustained—sustaining.

THESE LAST LINES—THE COUPLET, so to speak, of the unrhymed son-
net "Providence," commencing this remarkably varied selection—limn
the modus operandi of several poems, particularly in the first third of
An Evensong. To anatomize: Nathaniel Schmidt perceives "how our world
. . . alters" moment by moment; and his relentless rapid fire, rhythmic cata-
logues "Channel [his] wish to change" the observed phenomena in flux into
"aria[s—]sustained" for considerable length, as image after image is assimi-
lated. As, for example, in "Mother's Day Verse":

> . . . and so he came to a card-store, searching
>
> for a truer sentiment than what
>
> these mall-bags on his arm could say;
>
> their vermouth sweater of approximate size,
>
> random best-seller of presumed enjoyment,
>
> and pre-packaged brand-names sufficiently bold
>
> to boast of bank-statements to passing-by strangers

And so Schmidt goes on for three virtuosic stanzas, as "her son sought
a more sympathetic text, fore-ordained, 'just the right word.'" But though
the persona may search in vain for "a response . . . his gesture struggled to
comprehend,"[1] Schmidt's "Verse" itself *constitutes a soul sustaining aria*. The
same may be said for "Transcription," "Romantics," "'Wordhoard onleac,'"
"'. . . hovering over the deep,'" "E=MC²," and such like. These performance
pieces were composed somewhat under the sway of Hart Crane,[2] whose

---

1. The child in Billy Collins' "The Lanyard" fares better than this character—though
not the child become the man who speaks the poem and shares with Schmidt's "search[er]"
"the archaic truth / that you can never repay your mother." As for Collins and Schmidt:
the first's verse touches via humor, whereas "Verse" strikes by feverish intensity.

2. Schmidt's congeries, though also his method of assemblage, appear to correspond
with the products and practice underwritten by what Crane terms the "logic of metaphor

work Schmidt knows well and has written about expertly (I first met our poet in his critical capacity). Yet for all the disparate influences on his output, Nathaniel Schmidt sounds singularly—and again, variously.

Impressive as are these "arias," I prefer his series of ekphrastic poems. That eye so attuned to the 'altering world,' when fixed upon a tableaux, transmutes painting into speech analogously sensuous, colorful, and nuanced. From "On Salvador Dali's *The Sacrament of the Last Supper*":

Why is one wearing yellow?

Did the Teacher value him more, imputing some brilliance,

or, perhaps the better bet, has Judas allowed his coin-lust

to soil his clothes with a urine hue?

Who can tell, when outside, diamonds rise as mountains,

defining this holiscape?

This sight, seamlessly disappearing like ether,

In "After Paul Reuben's *The Rape of the Daughters of Leucippus*," "I observe two mythical women, manhandled, *denuded by paint*" (italics mine) indexes the pinpoint accuracy of Schmidt's depiction of the *other* artist with *his* medium *attiring nakedness*. This savage poem upon a savage theme is superscribed—i.e., not with an epigraph but situated above the title—with the dictate from Genesis 3:15: "And you will strike his heel." And indeed, overarching the collection, as the appellation *Evensong* portends, is the sacrament. At times, its investiture is intimated, as in the plaintive, poignant, grotesquely beautiful "Indifference":

A nest of intestines lies beside the roadway,

knotted, contorted, cold, its contents

pulled by worn tires into cross-patterned stripes

along the pavement; almost half a doe,

her backside, tethered by a semi-smashed spine,

discarded behind some fall-altered shrubs.

. . . organically entrenched in pure sensibility," whereby "the terms of expression employed are often selected less for their . . . literal significance than for their associational meaning." Although it must be said that on the whole, even when so engaged Schmidt impresses as more conventionally logical (i.e. comprehendible) than Crane, and less 'purely' figurative—that is, Schmidt's images denote actual objects as well as metaphors for these objects. (Cf. Crane, "General Aims and Theories," and his letter to Harriet Monroe, rpt. in *Modern Poetics*, ed. James Scully [New York: McGraw-Hill, 1965] 153-64.)

For weeks, realtors, writers, parents and police
continue their journeys, determined, past this corpse
where even odd crows, who once sang their thanks
off-key like a suburban congregation,
have moved on to more popular communions,
but still, despite this demise, the beast's velvet tongue
graciously hangs from her delicate mouth,
panting for a stream she is impotent to find,
to whisper to the masses rushing onward,
How many more deaths must you dismiss every day?

More often, the sacramental vision is pronounced:

Pentecost

My God, my God, why hast thou forsaken me?

I do not know why the young man, grungy,
mounts himself high on the bridge's hand-rail,
the courthouse-clocktower's shadow looming
over squad-cars barricading the street
while I drive to a Good Friday service,

but he intends to soar like Pegasus
until gravity makes him Icarus,
a hopeless fiction crushing his temple
when he strikes on the pavement I travel.
Excusing myself, I hurry ahead

to say *Mea culpa! Mea culpa!*
before our redemptive relic, tortured,
yearning for love while failing to provide,
praying, a poor Samaritan, for a ghost,
guardian, uniformed, blue, who will say:

I am with you always, to the very end of the age.

Ego vobiscum sum omnibus diebus usque

ad consummationem saeculi.

ἐγὼ μεθ᾽ ὑμῶν εἰμι πάσας τὰς ἡμέρας

Hey buddy. You okay? Come away so we may talk.

Here, as when the last eight lines of "The Ælf-Lord" are set in Saxon strong-stress alliterative meter, Schmidt in a sense 'retreats,' so literally *to speak* in an earlier idiom where belief remains enwoven in the words. He instances what Eliot terms (and what Schmidt's favorite poet, Seamus Heaney, cherished and practiced) "the auditory imagination":

> the feeling for syllable and rhythm, penetrating far below the conscious levels of thought and feeling, invigorating every word; sinking to the most primitive and forgotten, returning to the origin and bringing something back, seeking the beginning and the end. . ., fus[ing] the old and obliterated and the trite, the current, and the new and surprising, the most ancient and the most civilized mentality.[3]

In addition to the passage remarking verbal music, which Schmidt so sensitively intones, Eliot also underscores *return*, "bringing something back." Hence above, I qualified Schmidt's withdrawal, since that is always for him a stratagem of reconnaissance. Certain poems enact faith assaulted, questioned, yet vigilantly, doggedly retained, affirmed. And so his lyric "After Philip Larkin," forming one strain in a contrapuntal fugue with that great skeptic poet's "Church Going" and "High Windows," closes on "notic[ing] the Beauty in the bright-lighted windows, which is nothing, and yet something, and a mystery."[4] Yet one might contrast this credo reticently

---

3. T.S. Eliot, *The Use of Poetry and the Use of Criticism* ([1933] Cambridge: Harvard UP, 1961) 111. Heaney quotes Eliot at the outset of "Englands of the Mind," and elaborates: "I presume Eliot was thinking here about the cultural depth-charges latent in certain words and rhythms, that binding secret between words in poetry that delights not just the ear but the whole backward and abysm of mind and body: thinking of the energies beating in and between the words that the poet brings into half-deliberate play; thinking of the relationship between the word as pure vocable, as articulate noise, and the word as etymological occurrence, as symptom of human history, memory and attachments." (Seamus Heaney, *Preoccupations* [New York: Farrar, Straus and Giroux, 1980] 150.)

4. "Bright-Lighted Windows (after Philip Larkin)," ll. 19-20. To Schmidt's "somewhere," "High Windows" parries "nowhere"; and in place of "mystery," Larkin ends on "endless." Even so (and correlation of the texts brings out the point), Larkin's tone, *because* agnostic, harbors hope. And so also does "Church Going," "Since someone will

expressed to the "b[l]oom[ing]" avowal when Schmidt "Channels" the energetic overflow of his inner Hart Crane:

Covenantal

After Isaiah 55

Beneath the skull's overcast dome, a Farmer plows my brainfield
    with crooked, meandering, furrows, dusty trenches thirsting
like finches freshly hatched, featherless, whose radish-resembling heads
    instinctively anticipate what host a mother's beak may bring,
breadcrumbs, rose-buds, myrtle-sprigs, some writhing,
      shriveling, worm,
    want and provision erecting young necks from the nest,
its wattle fence their first exposure to faith, a forum for voicing
    psalms and complaints to the descending parent.

Like these chicks, my soil accepts whatever is planted, uncomprehended,
    blossoming sprouts up toward the sun while imaginative rains
baptize root-balls to tunnel down deep, universally feeding
    the sapling green limbs and heart-piercing thorns of figs and weeds
entangling this plot. Only the Gardener's keen shears can cultivate
    this fated harvest – prudence blooming its womb with a promise.

The projective force of the sonnet, its dense train of figuration, compound words, and sentiment summon comparison to one more poet in Schmidt's pantheon, Gerard Manley Hopkins, SJ.[5] And by the time these pages reach

---

forever be surprising A hunger in himself to be more serious, And gravitating with it to this ground" (ll. 59-61). And again, "Bright-Lighted Windows" sheds light on this predilection, via the respective poems' similar scenarios: in both texts, the speaker's diffidence transforms into respect.

5. The *patterned* energy Schmidt here presents may be construed in Hopkins' terms as a complicated *inscape* (since several objects comprise the "individually distinctive" "Oneness" of the scene) kept in being by the *instress* of "God's will through all things, which (i.e., the instress) additionally "carries the inscape whole into the mind of the perceiver." (*Gerard Manley Hopkins, Poems and Prose*, sel. And ed. W.H. Gardner [New York: Penguin, 1953] xx-xxiii; *The Princeton Encyclopedia of Poetics*, ed. Alex Preminger

his readers, the author may be enrolled in seminary. But as for likening his poetry to others, I have purposed to point up not only the proficiency of Nathaniel Schmidt, but, again, his singularity also. As T.S. Eliot observed (and who better to have *the* last word), a truly "Individual Talent" manifests as such only against the backdrop, and in the context, of "Tradition."

Dr. Ethan Lewis
University of Illinois Springfield
July, 2016

---

and T.V.F. Brogan [1993] 609.)

Acknowledgements and Notes

Beckwith Hills CRC – Beacon: For the Beloved

The Penwood Review: The Art Museum

Perspectives: Profession, Romantics, Transcription, "What is man that thou art mindful of him"

Sanskrit: Maud and the Swan

Time of Singing: Bright-Lighted Windows

Windhover: "Do this in remembrance of me", Edenic, The Converts, The Host

The 55 Project: Covenantal

This collection's epigraph is from G.K. Chesterton's *The Everlasting Man*.

Transcription alludes to lines and characters from *Beowulf*.

Mother's Day Verse alludes to the writings of Virgil and St. Augustine.

For the Beloved is for Gary and Anne.

"Wordhord onleac" takes its title from line 259 in *Beowulf*.

Profession responds to Job 13:15 (KJV).

$E=MC^2$ took its inspiration from Albert Einstein's essay of the same name.

Content is an ekphrastic poem written in response to Édouard Manet's famous painting, *Le Déjeuner sur l'herbe* (The Luncheon on the Grass).

Romantics contains ekphrastic elements engaging both Alphonse Mucha's painting *Spring* and Gustav Holst's orchestral suite *The Planets, Op. 32 –IV Jupiter, the Bringer of Jollity.*

The Ælf-Lord is for those students who shared their histories with me, and alludes to various fairy-stories, including those of C.S. Lewis, J.R.R. Tolkien, and Brian Jacques, while also utilizing the form and phrasing of the Anglo-Saxon poems *The Wanderer* and *Deor.*

"Do this in remembrance of me" is an ekphrastic poem on Salvador Dali's painting *The Sacrament of the Last Supper.* The title comes from Luke 22:19 (NIV).

"What is man that thou art mindful of him?" takes its title from Psalm 8:4 (KJV).

The Cave was written in response to Plato's famous allegory of the same name, and was inspired by a friend's work experience.

Pentecost quotes Matthew 27:46 (KJV) and Matthew 28:20 (NIV). Thank you to Jonathan Fischer and Rick Pinckney for their help with the Greek.

". . . hovering over the deep" paraphrases Genesis 1:2 (NIV) for its title.

Covenantal was composed in response to Isaiah 55.

On the St. John's Bible,/loaned to the college/where I teach, learn is an ekphrastic poem responding to the Heritage Edition of the illuminated Saint John's Bible which was loaned to the Hugh and Edna White Library at Spring Arbor University.

Syntax references Lord Byron's *Prometheus* and Percy Bysshe Shelley's *Prometheus Unbound.*

War on the Homefront is for all my military students.

Bright-Lighted Windows is a response poem to Philip Larkin's poems *High Windows* and *Church Going.*

On Criticism was inspired by images and philosophy mentioned in Jacques Derrida's essay "Force and Signification," while also working with ideas from Friedrich Nietzsche. The final stanza uses a line from Percy Bysshe Shelley's sonnet *Ozymandias*.

"And you will strike his heel" is an ekphrastic poem responding to Peter Paul Reuben's painting *The Rape of the Daughters of Leucippus*. Its title derives from Genesis 3:15 (NIV).

Maud and the Swan reimagines the poet W.B. Yeats' relationship with Maud Gonne in the context of Yeats' sonnet *Leda and the Swan*.

"Deliver us from Evil" takes its title from Matthew 6:13 (NIV), while its epigraph is from William Wordsworth's sonnet *The World Is Too Much With Us*.

Regeneration contains ekphrastic elements engaging *The Winged Victory of Samothrace, The Venus De Milo,* and *Pysche Revived by Cupid's Kiss*, all of which are housed in The Louvre.

Scripture quotations marked (NIV) are taken from the Holy Bible, New International Version®, NIV®. Copyright © 1973, 1978, 1984, 2011 by Biblica, Inc.™ Used by permission of Zondervan. All rights reserved worldwide. www.zondervan.com The "NIV" and "New International Version" are trademarks registered in the United States Patent and Trademark Office by Biblica, Inc.™

Scripture quotations marked (KJV) are from the King James Version of the Bible.

After God, of whom I cannot say enough, I must thank my parents, for without your continued sacrifice, teaching, encouragement, and love this project never would have come to fruition. Likewise, to my dearest Lydia, your love, support, and patience routinely incarnate the grace of Christ in my life. To Ethan Lewis (love with all due respect), I am forever indebted to our friendship – few have influenced my mind and art as much as you. I cherish our conversations. To David Urban, you taught me so much about our Lord, the pursuit of excellence, robust thinking, and the joy of the Word. I miss your classes. To Lew Klatt, your friendship, verse, and instruction have challenged and shepherded my imagination. You gave me the best assignment I ever received. To Gary Schmidt, you saw something before I ever did – it's a blessing being a Saint. Thank you for sharing your gifts. To Nancy Hull, as I prepared this manuscript, I fondly recalled watching you edit *On Rough Seas* and how you took a fledging poet under your wing during Saints. To Michael Stevens (Bro M.), you are the great encourager. So much good work has been produced thanks to your steadfast devotion to the words of others. To Jeffrey Bilbro, you are a true cultivator of words and the best of colleagues. To Kimberly Moore-Jumonville, thank you for the opportunity to teach, and for your unflinching encouragement of my work. To Nathaniel Hansen, thank you for being so selfless as you shared writing and reading opportunities. To Dave Harrity, you are a remarkably generous man who truly manifests the Image. Thank you for your invaluable criticism, counsel, and encouragement. To all of those not mentioned at Calvin College, the University of Illinois Springfield, Spring Arbor University, Jackson College, and Grace College, thank you for the education and employment that have helped to produce this collection. Likewise, to all my students, friends, and family who poured their lives into mine, thank you for your grace. To Matthew Wimer and everyone at Resource Publications and Wipf and Stock—thank you for making this book a reality. Lastly, thank you, dear reader.

Providence

Before shaping with your cheeks, tongue, teeth, lips
    the elements you blow through your larynx
to sing, expelling from within your lungs
    toxins, carbons, and sensitive pitches,
andante, allegro, pianissimo,
    their tensions, resolutions, conducting
the melodies passing through your organs
    to disturb the stagnant air, to create:

breathe. Feel oxygen exalt your ribcage.
    Taste evergreens nourished by morning rains.
Inhale what lilies' leaves have cleansed, prepared,
    so blood can feed muscles with airborne spirits.
      Channel how our world you wish to change alters
        so you might proclaim your aria, sustained—sustaining.

Transcription

Let us romanticize a monk, hunched-over, candle-lit,
   a sackcloth habit snuggled close
      to repel the winds besieging his abbey, medieval, dark,
his stylus tracing pregnant sounds, presumably Latin,
   though perhaps Greek, Hebrew, some proto-dialect,
      or the heathen's vocabulary in their stories he loves,
Grendel, demonic, of the line of Cain,
   one tale redeemed by the one he believes
      which questions if Unferth, kith-killer, is beast or man.
This ink stands opposite the page, black versus white,
   and yet our grey-cells imagine colour,
      the flame's soft glow, an icicle's depth, blood's red,
trusting that symbols represent, that meaning resides somewhere,
   compelling us all to speak from the heart,
      that timeless entity ruled by reason (or so we think)
to read our vast world like a book, each character
   at work, every school-day's play-script, erotic dramas,
      and history's liturgies, both sacred and secular,
stimulants derived from outside ourselves, random or determined,
   that demand we respond to this old scribe's conviction
      that he merely reflects a superior poet
whose work is a vivid illumination, unfathomable.

Foreign

Only 15, the Mayo dew moistening the heath,
I passed through a pub's vestibule to the gents
to tap a kidney before others on our tour
imbibed their pints; Seans and Patricks
born in Detroit, Philly, manifesting
their culture's dictations of our lineage,

and I unzipped my machine-stitched fly
to relieve what my body produced,
the ale-colored stream pouring into
a familiar porcelain sleeve uniquely shell-shaped
with brass-fittings patinaed sea-green.

Here, in the county of my foremother's birth,
someone's grand-da shuffled past me
and rested his shaky hand by a urinal
where the wainscoting, stained mulberry and moss, was worn;
resilient silver hairs wrestling free from his cap
as a peat-dyed sweater held snugly loose skin.

Tá sé fuar go leor ínnio
trickled across his tongue
(or so I presume), shocking my eyes ajar
and away as if they'd spied on some moonlit shore
a seal step out from its flecked, pebble-pale, coat
to expose a colleen's glistening contours—a selkie.

Agch, gleamed his cracked lips, *you must be American.*

Failte.

Mother's Day Verse

... and so he came to a card-store, searching
for a truer sentiment than what
these mall-bags on his arm could say;
their vermouth sweater of approximate size,
random best-seller of presumed enjoyment,
and pre-packaged brand-names sufficiently bold
to boast of bank-statements to passing-by strangers
each unable to articulate what his psyche felt
needed to be uttered to an aging mother.

Surrounded by similar gentlemen,
his fingers fluttered through the vast offering
as she must have done back in college
when she scavenged the library's catalogue
for commentaries on Dido's despair
that discussed how gilt mosaic couches, pleasurable caresses,
and tongue-woven soliloquies failed
to persuade Aeneas to remain by her side
when the gods had decreed their division,

although her son sought a more sympathetic text,
fore-ordained, "just the right word,"
in this gallery of glitter, clichés, and cartoons
to worship her decades of sacrifice,
her changing diapers by the crib at 3,
a healthy diet of tales not always desired,
and the "ambassador speech," her prayer
reminding him of what he'd been taught, whose he was,
whenever he went out into the world;
each of these and more demanding a response
even if his gesture struggled to comprehend.

For the Beloved

When the casket stands open   and the mourners arrive,
  scarves round their necks,   fingers at their eyes,
utterance fails.
God may have created   by the word of his power
  and given dear Adam, firstborn,   direction to define,
    rhinoceros, hippopotamus,   platypus, tigress,
      even "flesh of my flesh,"   Eve,
        whose daughter now rests   in that mahogany bed,
but this is unnatural.
Stopped lies the tongue,   lifeless, rigid, and dry,
  for what does one say   when an infinite mind
    is reminded of time?:   the look first exchanged, his chattering knees,
      her preceding shy "Yes"   to their Holy witnessed "I do,"
        their enduring patience,   all ears filled with cries,
          the product of their love,   children now with children,
            who today say "Hello"   to those bidding "Farewell"
              —small solutions to the problem   "It can not be good
for man to be alone."
So why do I verse?   My song will not raise the dead;
  the chaotic void's gape   redevouring our world.
Such babbling proves bizarre,   like a prophet's strange vision,
  though perhaps just as vital,   for it confesses a belief
    in the Word's existence,   capable of redeeming
      what we sense is immortal,   whose incarnate Voice wept
        at Lazarus's tomb,   Sin's lingering shrill hiss,
          our soul's greatest fear,   rendered mute by the Speaker,
comforting.

"Wordhord onleac"

"[He] unlocked his word-hoard"—*Beowulf,* 259

Throned on a library's fifth floor
exalted over Midwestern farms,
moldy pages transform spade-blades
to slice through my brain's musky sod.

These modern-day runes document
the contents of Nordic longships,
hoards, torqs, gospels inlaid with gold,
and their theft's tongs: coif-crushing swords,

cleavers museums now collect,
their tongue-shaped blades constructed
from multiple steel bars, carbon,
twisted together like hay-bales;

fire reforming them mutable;
oil-baths quenching their pounded shapes
to etch serpentine coil-patterns
the breath of their divisive nibs.

Heirlooms, true edges prove treasures,
multiple elements melted
to produce one unbreaking form,
for single iron shards will shatter

against skulls encased in dense helms,
and my search uncovers artifacts,
weak beliefs hacked down in their prime,
as abandoned standards litter the earth

to sow relics in intellects,
mined and refined into ingots;
the hazardous dross smelted off
to forge ploughshares reaping our grains.

Profession

After Job 13:15

"Though He slay me, still will I trust Him,"
   seems a rhetorical boast, easily made,
for who can comprehend this claim's worth
   when even at funerals, death remains abstract?
Yes, a tangible corpse lies stiff, dressed, and prone
   in a woodcrafter's pride, next hoisted
by dove-feigning fingers in soft cotton gloves
   onto broad shoulders, who then carry this cross
out to the hearse, to the church, to the earth,
   where, seed-like, it is planted,
expecting a glorious spring-rise,
   but these are effects, not the passing itself.
Does the soul feel anything during this procession?
   Who can say? Our sensations are those of the living.
The centurion's slave, when reanimated by Christ,
   neglected to mention his terrors and joys
when his eyes, like candles, were snuffed out by last breath,
   and nothing compelled his Savior to retell
his time down in Hell, let alone in High Heaven,
   outside of weeping and gnashing, splendor and grace.
Even nihilists imagine an eternity devoid
   of all sense, so small is their understanding of death.
Separation is the dagger that pierces in the dark,
   that thorn in the flesh coaxing out this sharp wail
"Though He take my first love, still will I trust Him,"
   fathoming the depths of devotion.

E=MC²

Condensed within an explosion of hair
and a sweater, his imagination
felt flesh and wool rub against soft leather
as he eased himself into a stuffed chair,
a warming sensation much like the match
he struck on his shoe-sole, friction sparking
energy, heat, light, and ability
so bold Prometheus's gift could be
applied to the elements of Nature,
tobacco shriveling inside his pipe,
atoms rearranging into gasses
that dispersed, expanded, and continued
observed as rich, calming, smoke floating free
like nebulae transversing throughout space,
the Pillars of Creation, still contained
by the weight of their source, gravity, time.

The cosmos preserves its own mass, power,
constantly balancing their scales justly.

Inside a middle-school, a half-grown child
slinks to the library and not the playground
after striking his brain-flint on Homer
to learn how both Achilles and Hector
perished because Paris could not control
his impulses, regardless of merit,
wishing the boys who had seen puberty
would not notice Odysseus wins,

and here, shielded by History's verse,
Caesar, Bonaparte, Tolkien, Derrida,
he starts interpreting a thick textbook
outlining elemental mechanics,
how we did not invent the atom bomb,
but merely posited a paradox
to Earth, *Abide by your laws or die,*
exercising the dominance we crave
with attempts to annihilate matter
in thoughts, words, and deeds, vast temples leveled
by unrelenting waves of wrath and flame.

From his office overlooking a lake,
a professor ponders these two thinkers
and the dense planet to which they are held,
their journeys in orbit around a source,
itself governed by celestial slaves,
the Sun, Moon, Jupiter's multiple priests,
each pulling, responding, to positions,
electrons to the nucleus of Life,
and our philosopher wonders at this:

Do other-worldly planes suspend our sphere,
we the fulcrum for dimensions, morals,
total, absolute, depravity, good,
unperceived realms of intangible heft?
Do they conspire and war to correct
us from stumbling into daemons and gods,

language the result of a tower,
stars burning bright to grant grace to prophets,
a virgin's womb spontaneously ripe
because sons will intentionally spoil,
and does everything signify vectors
emitting from a point still unwitnessed
in a black hole's concentrated abyss;
did All-That-Is once breathe *Let there be light*?

Content

After Édouard Manet's *Le Déjeuner sur l'herbe*
(The Luncheon on the Grass)

What naked truth stares overtly at us
   as we continue to discuss our day's controversies,
perhaps politics, ethics, or the current aesthetic,
   the importance of canes or the most proper coat-cut,
gesticulated words of unheard significance
   which led our subject to discard
her virginal blue gown, woven straw hat, and lunch's apples
   with hopes of attracting some third eye,
her life-giving breasts in full season
   just waiting to be plucked from her chest,
and yet neither her friend nor companion will have her,
   boring the revealed to look outside her time
where we gawk without shame at this neatly framed scene?
   Perhaps her display will make us consider her sister,
younger, restrained, less noticed in the garden's distance,
   trying to bathe clean some unwitnessed stain
from her shift, more domestic, unOlympian, real,
   subtly enticing us to invite her back home
and carefully uncover her glistening skin, engaged.

Pygmalion

You know not Byron, nor Auden, nor Yeats, nor Donne
(whose books inhabit my bedroom's planed shelves)
penned this poem you now read—for it recalls
my tweed coat slumped over my armchair
where I sit writing behind my roll-top;
a ceramic statue I painted perched
atop this desk as Apollo, my pet parrot,
repeats whistles I sang into his cage:
I unable to create except in my own image.

Reflecting, a Norton Anthology
reminds as I toil of Pygmalion,
his hammering's *ting-ding* cadence resounding
on the chisels chipping away all day
at shadowless marble, blank like vellum.

Each blow strips a piece of concealing stone
to reveal proportions complimenting
this sculptor's perceptions, what he loves most,
her shoulders, slender neck, braided hair bun,
and fine hands, one outstretched, one on her naked thigh,
all fashioning what he finds to be beautiful,

and when he is finished, her shape formed *good*,
he collapses to the ground where she stands
to wash the dust from her feet, worshipping
this manifestation of his vision
separated from his flesh like an amputated rib.

Do his Creators (who molded his genome's play-script)
now descend from Olympus to cleanse his brow
and animate his work with their breath,
like you do my verse, tongues shaping the air
to fill lungs with life, the Divine's medium?

The Art Museum

With frazzled mothers, smug-faced lawyers, waist-high scholars, and sirens
wearing stockings,
the poet me is pulled beyond the doors flung open like a book
to encounter the lovely ladies, either young or aged-wise, welcoming our
city
with stickers and a smile, directing us toward vital lines
made pragmatically novelesque as they guide through stacks of paper,
floor-plan upon floor-plan,
while others, more poetic, shade the wall-hung vellums true
with graphite, ink, and charcoal musings
to mirror the soul's vast palette repeatedly to the masses.

Tenderly, a broad-shouldered savior carries a balloon out of doors
so its previous small custodian need not witness its final breath,
and here, east of Eden, this building becomes important,
the half-filled shrines of industry having sacrificed their faithful
so that a father, for the rent, will gladly sketch my portrait
as a cellist hopes that Chopin has a following on the streets
where a starving toothless veteran prays that God will send a friend,

while back within, a naïve lamb innocently asks
Are we inside a church?

Romantics

He loosens his work-tie's noose-knot, ascending a staircase
  climbing above our grey earth, fallen leaves clotting gutters in the car-park
    where a divorced neighbor, half-lifed, drags on a cigarette,
      smoldering time until her bed-mate's pickup returns,
        a faded T-shirt her smock, her hair a mess like a nest.
Exhausted, Ulysses stumbles into his haven, a two-room apartment,
  having passed by the taupe vestibule's Charybdis, its mailbox,
    filled with bills starving for their pounds of flesh,
      to behold as he does every morning and evening
        Mucha's print *Spring* watching over his kitchen.
Within this nymph's bower, life flames eternal, a cherry-tree's
  rouge growing out of her skin, her bosom's furnaced gleam
    glowing through her sheer shift as blossom-crowned tresses,
      a Promethean grace, encompass, though not consume, what is immortal;
        neither hair nor limb broken, merely bent, under pressure.
Her mystique enthralls visions as he kicks off his shoes,
  the stereo serving Holst like a sherry, Jupiter's strings fluttering
    through his conscious, stately poise and grandeur exercising restraint
      for a movement, cheer trumpeting forth next with tambourine timbre
        to chase after dryads, nyads, and notes, emphatically, triumphantly,
        grand,
a pursuit he indulges until sun-up, where, with coffee in hand,
  he chars into embers, alone, Virginian and Latakian leaves,
    transforming their death into a creamy, cool, smoke,
      his pipe far finer than what the next-door Juno tries to quit,
        their ritual sacrifice struggling to conserve what they cherish.

The Converts

The trench-coated Dalí-man,
    his cortex soiled by thunderstorms
    to run subreally down,
fled the heaven-born critic's flood
    by diving into an old bookshop
    where Rousseau, Thoreau, and even Christ
irrigated senses with potent smells
    —all second-hand and supposed rot—
    to shelter his now humbled form
with lies or latent truths.
    What struggles will survive this night
    like each before and since?
I wondered from my poet's corner
    while the weary shop-keep considered Bach
    better than the playing Brahms
—uncertain how one was restored
    when this stranger saw a faded print
    nailed above the entrance door:
our Madonna's nipple on her infant's tongue.

The Ælf-Lord

Throned high upon a rosewood rocking chair
my cardiganed father would sit beside my bed
most twilights of my adolescent season
and recite from paperbacks fantasies
to spellbind my malleable mind
before he and my mother would commend my soul
in darkness to their prayers and my dreams.

Wild, prerequisite voices summoned shades
of beavers prophesying about winter's end,
centaurs reading stars to discover a returning king,
and of a kilted squirrel who slew his culture's dragon
—an adder—with an antique rune-gilt sword
to imitate ballads lauding a noble heir
who thawed his betrothed's stone-encrypted heart
with the warmth of his promissory kiss.

Rarely, today, do I hear such tales sung
as I assess the inevitable essays
one receives as an English professor:
memoirs of how indignant fingers pulled her panties down
(let us stop. . . like he did not—she was but a child),
of daughters flinching like finch-pinched worms
after storms because they failed to understand divorce,
a father-pressured abortion, a mother's death,
or of the narcissistic drivel the naïve spout
about their greatness, presumed paychecks, and worlds without pain.

Have not all these stories shaped my definitions,

their languages teaching my imagination

how to speak about my Lord, and to him,

as I now sound like an Old English wanderer?:

Where is the master of verse-craft?   Where is his saga of hope?

Where the unbroken shield-word?   Where the raiment of thought?

They have passed like breath from our rib-grove,   like smoke from
*   the hearth,*

floating from book-halls and mead-stores   along the heathers and fjords

for our kith no longer keep kin,   our eyes caught up by fame-hoards
*   and lusts,*

although like the moon falls and rises,   like the summer that follows
*   frozen nights,*

these too shall pass,   I believe like the bards before me,

if we boast to our maidens and sons   that a listening king still whispers.

"Do this in remembrance of me"

After Salvador Dalí's *The Sacrament of the Last Supper*

He looks nothing like what I expected,
clean-shaven, golden-haired, more like
Sigurd or Apollo than anything
encountered in a Midwestern Sunday School room,
and he starts turning transparent,
a vessel resting on a tranquil lake
nestled within his soon pierced side,
while on the table welcoming us home
bread, broken like the sacrificed lamb
Abraham passed through to sign God's covenant,
leads up to a cup accepting life-blood.

No one looks at him, save us,

now distracted to study twelve mystics
robed in glittering linens.
Each gazes at the ground, head bent, silent,
appearing statuesque on his clerical knees
while all meditate rather than feast.
Why is one wearing yellow?
Did the Teacher value him more, imputing some brilliance,
or, perhaps the better bet, has Judas allowed his coin-lust
to soil his clothes with a urine hue?

Who can tell, when outside, diamonds rise as mountains,

defining this holiscape?
This sight, seamlessly disappearing like ether,
recenters our eyes on the luminous son
pointing to whom he submits,
himself, and yet not himself,
those long exposed arms heavenly outstretched
to hover above our world's small waves;
his monolithic structure firmly in place,
almost invisible at our level.

Autumnal Landscape

The empty-nester crunches her brush's thistle
against canvas, reconceiving with ocher,
cadmium, lapis lazuli, a Michigan home-town
constructed alongside a river's dam, remodeling
as she stands within a park, engulfed
by mums, maples, and benches dedicated to spouses,
techniques her instructor executes
every Thursday evening at 5
("now that Helen has gone off to State")
right down to the cotton cover-all
and swan-winged glasses her classmates find peculiar.

Lydia, my college-met ladyfriend, joins me to peer
over her shoulder, wondering how well she is doing.
Do the ripples of the fall
bubble and froth with acceptable ferocity
to disperse the salmon fly-fishermen seek,
and are the shadows faithfully washed
on a toddler's cheek after his ice-cream has spilled,

or do we perceive, barely,
the hint of a glinting iris
on the surf colored blonde by the sun,
this body surging forth toward tributaries
where the leafy limbs of a long-rooted willow
lift from the current on the breeze?

"What is man that thou art mindful of him?"

What do we mean when we say children are God's artistry
as preachers are want to do during baptisms,
deleting from their homilies words like "daughter" and "girl"
as they exhort their faithful not to deface her beauty?

Her cries, while precious, necessary, compelling her mother
from tranquil acceptance to energized aid in the nursery,
are hardly melodic like deft little fingers
dropped by a pianist on his Steinway, the right hand
aware of what the left, separate, is doing,
darting playfully after a soprano's coy scales
as an orderly bass-clef foundations this sanctuary, physical, real.

Infantile outbursts for food and cleansing,
though expressive, honest, fail in comparison to a reserved recital,
and likewise, the Whitman-resembling Monet's impressions
of water-lilies inspire far more than photographs
spontaneously captured on a walk through the park,
one an orchestrated cacophony of color,
pinks, lavenders, oranges, and blues, what we enjoy,
care for, remember most, intangible
light-rays lingering in a dimly viewed mirror,
the other a firm fact snatched abruptly from history.

These bright clumps of paint teach what the blind man believed,
what, in juvenile terms, exhausted, his soul truly loved,
compulsory observations revealing a pregnant body
which reminds he, like us, the photographers, was conceived,
our complex capacity for creation intimating an unseen Father.

The Cave

In windowless cubicle-land, 2 shades of grey,
a woman with fizzy match-head-like hair
stares without blinking
at images
projected on a computer's square screen,
using words like *cutting, splicing, blending*
to process what she is doing:
speaking with button-clicks
to something that only responds
to 1's & 0's, on's & off's, change,
developing the evening's newsreel.

She crafts her video's syntax,
outlining the invention of two men
who constructed with screws and nails
(stewed in a pressurized cooker)
a paralyzing sphere of light and sound;
their bomb's dust eclipsing a Boston sidewalk
and its pageantry of flags, barricades, marathoners,
and humanoid shapes dispersing like roaches.

Simply, she casts shadows of their deed.
Omitted are the vacancies
painting the pavement a wet red,
the fullness of a stroller
tipped over, abandoned, solitary,

the screams too comfortable here,
and every clip deleted because it might scar a retina
like her own, unable to close tonight:

interning some home-bound widow in peace
as she settles in with her cats and left-overs,
though she fumbles to shut the family-room's blinds;
her fingers quaking at the report
her TV displays.

Edenic

When I realize I can never return;
when the scents of tulips and ferns
couple with breezes frolicking
along the collegiate fields
where we first reenacted Marlowe's
passionate nymphal enticements,
ravishing my nostrils with memories
so that my lungs desire to expand
beyond their ribcage's constraints;
when I know that the hourglass
can never be righted
for its sands continue to pile
moment upon moment upon moment;
how we are so naïve, unaware,
that we should appreciate, enjoy,
each experience before it drops down
the perpetual bottleneck of Time
like a phrase now already spoken;
I reimagine from my dreams a chapel
anchored to a vast gothic church.
Elizabethan, expansive,
pewless, and studious,
having one solid door, high windows,
and hearth-flames vigorously dancing
like dryads on Midsummer's Eve,
it is ringed by bookcases
keeping copious old friends
who will snuggle with you

while the sun and the moon
indulge their pursuit
—and you are there, clothed,
your beautiful calves peeking out
from beneath your skirt-hem,
and you smile at me, contentedly,
as God must have done
when He said "It is good"
as we stand alongside one another
and descend to our knees and pray.

Pentecost

My God, my God, why hast thou forsaken me?

I do not know why the young man, grungy,
mounts himself high on the bridge's hand-rail,
the courthouse-clocktower's shadow looming
over squad-cars barricading the street
while I drive to a Good Friday service,

but he intends to soar like Pegasus
until gravity makes him Icarus,
a hopeless fiction crushing his temple
when he strikes on the pavement I travel.
Excusing myself, I hurry ahead

to say *Mea culpa! Mea culpa!*
before our redemptive relic, tortured,
yearning for love while failing to provide,
praying, a poor Samaritan, for a ghost,
guardian, uniformed, blue, who will say:

I am with you always, to the very end of the age.
Ego vobiscum sum omnibus diebus usque
ad consummationem saeculi.
ἐγὼ μεθ' ὑμῶν εἰμι πάσας τὰς ἡμέρας
Hey buddy. You okay? Come away so we may talk.

". . . hovering over the deep"

Enlist your imagination, and bind it to the mast.
Heed my siren's call sung from the mizzen
and step your sole on this Nantucket craft,
a time-coursing vessel, her spars carved from oak ribs
pulled from Earth's side, copper skin clothing her bones
and your dust, the fetus soon sown inside her hold's belly,
so you both can odyssey from a shared birthplace
to discover doubloons, renown, harbors
with strangers who seek at world's end fortunes;
albatrosses orbiting the triune mastheads.

Do not forget the pagan harpooner, tattooed,
or the orphaned boy schooled by heathens to survive
when you enter in her captain's quarters,
endowed like Noah's ark with vital artifacts,
not pairs of elephants or kangaroos,
but what rests between the port-glasses and bread,
a sextant and compass joining the Eucharist
to help navigate the globe's circumstance,
while significantly, the ghosts of men
leave footprints in the sand on the pages of books
flanking the contemplative rear window
that watches our wake remembering this voyage.

Jonah, Columbus, Magellan, and whom you bring,
Melville, Crane, the charts and graphs from your life,
breach like Poseidon's hippocampi the mind's waves
to plot expeditions after new ports

we trust exist, faith justifying our struggle
against what currents churn in the impeding sea:
tides reaching out for the moon's pregnant womb,
the presumed dumb leviathan whale, wounded Ahab's foe,
singing fugues to its spouse on their sojourn,
the insidious schemes of kraken, Charybdis,
clacking their jaws to devour whom they may,
and the curses your crewmates spit out in the squall;
all affecting the weather outside our control.

Such sea-spay, salty, proves bountifully sound,
teaching why we pilot after fresh, tranquil, streams,
a trek that is governed by the heavens,
its polestar interpreted by the magi's inventions
so we might tread, as on a bridge, over the deep—
shimmering pools mirroring an intrepid Forefather.

Covenantal

After Isaiah 55

Beneath the skull's overcast dome, a Farmer plows my brainfield
    with crooked, meandering, furrows, dusty trenches thirsting
like finches freshly hatched, featherless, whose radish-resembling heads
    instinctively anticipate what host a mother's beak may bring,
breadcrumbs, rose-buds, myrtle-sprigs, some writhing, shriveling, worm,
    want and provision erecting young necks from the nest,
its wattle fence their first exposure to faith, a forum for voicing
    psalms and complaints to the descending parent.

Like these chicks, my soil accepts whatever is planted, uncomprehended,
    blossoming sprouts up toward the sun while imaginative rains
baptize root-balls to tunnel down deep, universally feeding
    the sapling green limbs and heart-piercing thorns of figs and weeds
entangling this plot. Only the Gardener's keen shears can cultivate
    this fated harvest—prudence blooming its womb with a promise.

The Host

Fingers, unnoticed, knead dough
into a clay-like consistency
created as though an alchemist's paste;
maize's mystery mortar and pestled
to be bathed in water ladled
from the brook where it once trickled
after the sun, our warmth-master,
lured and transfigured droplets
into sheer linens to adorn
the moon's matrimonial curves
and her fraternal constellations,
the hunter, the lion, two bears
who loomed their gaze over a doe
that lapped in some far away thicket
a stream coursing round ferny crags,
the fountain where rain first ascended.

See manipulated ingredients gleam
as the loaf, pulled from the oven,
cools to an ingestible temp,
fragrance enchanting the granite brick-work
to summon to the table souls
who temporarily tolerate transgressions,
those mallets, nails, and shovels
our hands and tongues do employ
to crucify neighbors for our gain

while we toil to satisfy hungers
beneath the ceiling we must share,
consuming our realm's rich bounty,
reformed, not destroyed, by flames.

Now imbibe the wine here offered
to alter your incarnate demeanor,
what conjugates your verb "to be"
into a state of affirmed existence,
and taste the vineyard's terroir,
its sea-salts, figs, apples, and oaks
subtly revealing their blessings
in the blood-colored fruit of the vine,
cultivated for generations
in California, Cologne, and Cana;
the soil to where we will return
used to encourage those reborn.

Mother Church

Consider the cockle in the mud, how
　　it toils, a pilgrim's symbol, receiving
specs of shale, sand, what dusts the currents send
　　into the dappled, bi-valve's cup, ribbed, wombed,

so its meat, mutable, can ruminate
　　like our brains on weird books, revelations,
to develop, responsively, with its object
　　a pearl, birthing from irritants—treasures.

What values does this mussel, now wived, lose
　　if we spoon from its shell-skull moist, grey, flesh,
separating, defining, its being
　　down like a daughter named only Body—Mind—Soul?

Is not her triune whole vital, essential, part
　　of our seabed's culture, what the Diver desires?

Phosphorescence

Store-front neons contribute their electric broadcasts
Kavanaugh's, Discounts, Cigars, Girls
to the glow radiating from skyscrapers,
remarkably brilliant with their shades of chartreuse, pearl,
that colonize the celestial night with their sceptered sheen,

and obscure what I want to behold,
starlight, the geometric points of heaven
that my imagination can connect to create
Orion, the hunter, my childhood hero,

and thus I abandon this eclipsed darkness
and cross the threshold of a steepled cathedral
positioned between insurers to the West
and soup-kitchens to the East.

Inside, on its ceiling's expanse,
painted an artificial blue,
I see constellations citizens had stenciled
to resemble *Ursa Minor* and her she-bear
who point out the polestar
guiding through pews paths to the chancel
where bread, like everything within this space,
imitates unseen realities.

An audience congregates:
fastidious grandmothers with rhinestones and spouses,
a lonely professor, bow-tied, in his best corduroy,

freshmen lovers dressed in their hoodies and bliss,
and children dragged in by their parents,
disorderly, brash, unlike the thawing homeless.

Then a boy-choir begins to sing,
converting a composer's inked dots and dashes
into physical thoughts that ripple the air,
the choristers adorned in white linen robes
imputed upon crimson-dyed cassocks

and each disciplined voice proclaims its part
in obedience to where their conductor directs,
their melodic pitches harmonizing in rhythms
of pleasurable ebbs that tremble eardrums,

rearranging faces in the assembled populace,
their pupils focused, foreheads unwrinkled, chins uplifted:
overtones swelling to quake my core

as if a sun had been birthed in some void,
a fiery eruption echoing in my physique
so I will tangent back into the evening,
glowing.

Joseph

She loves him more, I have no doubt,
    her incredible story proving this point;
those supple thighs, what I long to key, remaining padlocked
    while her heart, nestled within her bosom's crib, welcomes home Another.
She desires his will, her ears, and womb, filled with his Word,
    deaf to the snickers of *slut, whore,* and *cuckold fool.*
Oh why, when I'm willing to cherish, provide, does she surrender herself
    so fully to one whom I cannot see?

My thoughts must be true as her changed belly supports,
    though does "more" favor neutralize "less," does love hinder love?
Despite our neighborhood's talk, she lingers beside me here,
    and I notice her blue-eyed fear if I reject her son.
We can experience unity still though we hunger each ourselves.
    She hazards all for this child. I shall do the same.

On the St. John's Bible, loaned to the college where I teach, learn

A library's pinewood reliquary
            gave me witness

to the endowed ink-strokes
an artisan priest
                had serifed
with fluid motion

on the vellum my thumbs
longed, trembled, to touch

like the lover who lay
straight the flush thread
wedding each folio.

            A trinity of pigments
illuminated

a face mouthed by a cross
emerging
            from an abstract clay-wash,

blood-soaked, sun-burnt,
as charcoal orbits, soft eyes,

         watched over

rose-window shaped nets
resembling stars

in a sea of azure.

Here, a figure of gold (haloed),
his features undefined,

cast his hands above
            pisces
(radiant shadows like himself)

to bridge
     the vision on my right
     with the smoldering collage
on my left:

a crucible of umbered ash and blued ore

into which Pegasus
                        fell
and where Babylon's stallion
                        leapt
wingless, in vain,

with panicked lips
and gnashed teeth

for his rider was crushed, consumed,

under his throat.

                    Did I truly see

ON THIS ROCK
I WILL BUILD
MY CHURCH
AND THE GATES OF HELL
WILL NOT PREVAIL

                foundationed,
inscribed, on the oceans
                            while

YOU ARE THE MESSIAH,
THE SON OF THE LIVING
GOD
    was gold-leafed
on the human face
well-springing verses
across a tabula rasa?

If so, how could I divorce

from this vision
to dispense my day with silent grading,

unlike a student

who dashed
        to a table
of her fellow disciples,

blurting
They let me turn the page!

where it was written

SO THE LAST WILL BE FIRST
AND THE FIRST WITLL BE LAST

?

Reunion

Come here, little brother, away from the sow and her squealing sucklings
    before they trample all your uniformed men, those birthday presents
you entombed head-deep in some mud-fashioned forts, a lopsided empire
    revealing sunk talents in its broken construction,
and join us, little sister, in our house upon a cliff,
    a lighthouse you never need clean,
and do not worry about the state of your dress, its silk appears spotless
    in my eyes
    though I know where you slave in the dust.

Oh, my persistent young learners, how dimly you perceive the true cost
    I paid for the crossbeam supporting our estate,
crushed knuckles, twisted joints, cracked ribs, horrid sights,
    their unfestering scars still lingering on my skin,
that claywork reflection of my infinite faces
    I kilned to become like you—in need of a father

who ignites a bright flame in an exalted window
    so we can return home together.

Syntax

Remember Prometheus, flame-sparker,
his flesh bound by Olympian limits
to mountain crags, the titan observing
humanity fashioning shelters, plows,
with his metal-manipulating gift,
as well as other works, spears, xiphoi, knives;
ravens consuming his liver each day
while beating, bruising, about his eyebrows,
impairing his keen processing power
to punish the act of aiding vain us.

Did this story's character contemplate
if Zeus was ruled by the principles of hate
as the poets Byron and Shelley penned,
his immortal mouth not prophesying
about the godhead's demise out of spite,

or did he transcribe his native grammar
from Hellenistic myth to Hebraic?

Elijah fled the wrath of King Ahab
after foretelling of Baal's failure
to unlock the storm-cloud's grain-giving rain,
following YHWH's voice east to a wadi,
a cavernous ravine normally dry,
except this season, when streams sustained groves
and ravens, divine, airlifted livers, loaves,
to him who would not deny the Lord's love,

and did this archetype later confuse
when a carpenter's son would not refute
a question from Jove-worshipping Pilate,
Are you the king of the Jews?—his people
demanding the Quiet's crucifixion?

Did we then choose to impale Love's gut,
Son of God defined in the flesh of man,
so carrion lusters could hover nearby
as blood from our thorns pooled in his eyes
and baptized his perspective on our pride,
commending his soul to his father's care
while he asked Omnipotence to forgive?

War on the Homefront

As I commence teaching, of all things, Owen's *Dulce. . .*, this student
    recoils from his desk, his mind assaulted, regrouping
his sight invaded by an exposed power-outlet Maintenance neglected
    on the floor, blue and white wires tangled with carpet-tufts, an IED
for this Marine's veteran memory, what he aims to neutralize
    by dropping book-bags on this device, camouflaging wounds
like a tattoo-sleeve lays down cover over defacing shrapnel scars,
    but this scenario overwhelms, routing this husband, this father
      of a newborn,

from this classroom.
    A serviceman once told me "In Basic,
    this sergeant kills your word 'I,' replaces it with 'this recruit,'
and then orders this recruit to name what will care for him
    after what he cares for: this M-4 made Annie, Martha,
occupying this chamber beside his bed; his spouse—a utility,
    utility—sacrifice," and this professor crumbles at this language,
this vandalism, and so radios for reinforcements
    for what is human, what is holy.

The Angel of the Lord

Steam shimmers off evaporating snow
to conjure mirages between poplars
as I trudge through spring-signaling warmth
and wander beside a crystalline lake,

and transversing through time and books I see
scavenging Norse-folk with blonde-hair braided
digging for tubers on their fjord's hillside;
ravens circling over rough whale-roads.

What visions are received when they look out?
What does the imagination believe?
Like Odin, Wisdom's seeker, do they spy
Odin cloaked in fog, hat steepled, distant?

Thoughts do dwell in the mist, eliciting
trembling humankind respond in its heart,
the intellect's wergild justifying
a doubtful quest: *Who are you? Are you true?*

The Shape-Shifter's multiple monikers
make us question his will's integrity,
Giant-Slayer, All-Father, Deceiver;
these contradictions cleave his soul in two.

The Spirit lusting for blood, sacrifice,
ruling a culture of death, Ragnarok,
cannot be the God, martyred, spear-point pierced,
who let himself be hung on the World-Tree,

and I grapple with these solid shoulders
like Jacob through the night at Peniel,
Right's might crushing my presumptuous bones
until he blesses me with Valhalla.

Bright-Lighted Windows

After Philip Larkin

I sit in the back of a church,
composing new poems on the back of a bulletin
with a pen that I've pilfered from the offertory plate
while my buddy beside me
devours the old preacher's long-winded words
like they are manna sent down from High Heaven.
He eats this stuff up,
this righteous community,
both genuine and somehow maternal,
and if it were not for our friendship
I'd be sitting alone in my study,
the sacraments of tobacco and scotch
laid out on my desk for the taking.
This is hardly paradise.
If only I had a leather-bound journal
or a tool with a decent ink-flow
then perhaps this morning could be saved,
but then, as the organ continues its droning,
I notice the Beauty in the bright-lighted windows,
which is nothing, and yet something, and a mystery.

On Criticism

After Jacques Derrida

Having just read, my mind stumbles as it wanders
upon columns, Roman, marble, broken,
erected in a fig grove ancients sowed
in an Alpine ravine by a fresh stream;
vines climbing the Apollonian shrine
as I forsake a thicket to explore.

The temple's dome had collapsed long ago,
and yet, when I stand in the center of its form,
I can see up through the ruin's circle
infinite hues of rouge as the sun sets,
replaced by the moon's particular light
(diverse cycles in a unified day),

though here is more than what the ring cages.
Examination reveals sage craftsmen,
inferred, imagined, from their chisel-marks,
their force reducing massive, quarried, slabs
to demonstrate with reserve what they knew,
that the god of meter requires a home

more glorious than these relic remains.
Their populace gave this skeleton flesh,
brought bulls, strong, for sacrifice, lyres to play,

and fears, desires, to this oracle
chosen from a pantheon of idols
—I deduce as I gaze at the altar.

In the dust, I notice a mosaic,
a thousand glass fragments combining to depict
Actaeon's demise when he spied Diana,
the sun-god's twin, pure, bathing by flora,
his vision desecrating her chaste shape
to reduce him to a doomed stag's instinct,

and I realize I am no different
than the artist who well those passions read,
enticed like the hunter's gaze to linger
and then chased in heart from her sanctuary
to die in a Bacchanalian wood,
having glimpsed some reality of life.

Indifference

A nest of intestines lies beside the roadway,
knotted, contorted, cold, its contents
pulled by worn tires into cross-patterned stripes
along the pavement; almost half a doe,
her backside, tethered by a semi-smashed spine,
discarded behind some fall-altered shrubs.
For weeks, realtors, writers, parents, and police
continue their journeys, determined, past this corpse
where even odd crows, who once sang their thanks
off-key like a suburban congregation,
have moved on to more popular communions,
but still, despite this demise, the beast's velvet tongue
graciously hangs from her delicate mouth,
panting for a stream she is impotent to find,
to whisper to the masses rushing onward
How many more deaths must you dismiss every day?

"And you will strike his heel"

After Peter Paul Reuben's *The Rape of the Daughters of Leucippus*

From the solitary safety of a coffee-table art-book,
   I observe two mythical women, manhandled,
denuded by paint, their soft rose-petal pink
   rump-cheeks blushed as blood rushes
to points of injury with energy;
   sun-scorched males, intent on empire,
surrounding their prey with stallions and gods
   in a once lush garden no longer pastoral.

One daughter, her noble satin shift, golden,
   discarded like an afterthought,
defines her back muscles by clenching, arching
   against the dictating, unflinching, fingers
that grip her shoulder to unground her right hand;
   her blonde braids unwound, tangled,
as the half-naked man, bull-brawned, gazes
   at her tender gender she conceals from us.

She looks, however, with stronger horror
   at her sister, bare-breasted, suspended in air
between the barbarian's chest and his armored brother,
   mounted, who drapes his aorta-dyed cape
around her ripe thigh, resigning his object
   to whatever verb his penetrating stare conceives;
her vestal white garments all but slipped off
   as she touches a hand to his forearm's sinews.

Fatefully, erotic cherubs strive to bridle
    the abductors' chargers circling, rearing,
about these women who extend their free hands
    toward the dawnstar burning off evening's storm,
what uplifts the airborne's visage, palm unclasped,
    as her sibling parallels by averting her eyes,
defending her brow—these the mothers revered by Rome,
    whose offspring will kill a virgin's firstborn.

Maud and the Swan

After W.B. Yeats

She pulled her poet close,
her back against a tree, his hands upon her bodice.
If tomorrow will not remember then "Yes" for tonight.
He had been so persistent, his pen becoming large
and begging her for love, damning her for pride
(inconsiderate of fear),
making her mount upon his hips, lips nibbling at her neck
as she clenched his downy hair,
anticipation's passion swelling inside their persons
as her naked thighs fell open like a book upon its spine,
and he wrote his conscience there,

> giving her his knowledge
> with long strong steady strokes.

Did she see him as a god,

> like one of Agamemnon's,

or as a beast unleashed from Hades,

> devolving before her eyes;

Another watching down from Heaven,

> editing their work?

> *Oh, how was that night preserved*
> *contrary to her will?*

Epithalamium

The citadel's sandstone walls shone like gold
in the sun that rained rays on the valley
narrowly passing between two mountains,
their snow-cloaked cliffs carved from onyx and lime
standing opposed to the vernal ravine
teaming with lilies rushing falls nourished.

Built on a hill, I first spied the tower
ascending skyward above this fortress
that watched over the orchards and bazaars
lining pathways leading to its gatehouse,
its virgin-blue tiled parapets rumored
to keep an unseen king or his magi,

and such pageantry enchanted my dreams
like a child thirsting after mother's milk,
and when I imbibed this fantasy's breeze,
it surprised how it reminded of Earth's,
distilling ideally its elixirs
to intoxicate and revive my self.

As I journeyed nearer to this city,
ripe apples like rubies gleamed on their boughs
and even bruised bushels appeared velvet
when a raven-haired woman flitted by
the cinnamon, clove, perfumed merchant-stalls;
an ivy-stitched skirt darting about her bare feet.

The dainty gold chain embracing her nude torso,
the embroidered bouquets on her bosom,
suggested she knew this realm's mysteries,
and so I gave chase to clutch her bounties,
bounding like a stag through the market
until a lady's restrained voice arrested me.

Peasant, down in the dust, heed me, she said,
standing on the drawbridge to her haven,
this daughter who descended her father's staircase
robed in white linen, a thin purple veil
covering her hair that carried a crown
of three silver chords fixed with dove-like wings.

Though your wanderer's eye does not deserve it,
the princess continued, *permit my speech*
to pass into your thoughts, then heart, to move your arms
so all might see you take my hand in yours
before your fingers unlace my corset
and reveal the intricacies of my form.

On my mother's bed where I was conceived,
I shall dress your tongue with our people's hymns,
songs by shepherds, soldiers, orphans, widows,
saving their suffering's gall, their comfort's mulled wine,
to produce heirs for this kingdom we inherit:
the verse-feast we shall share when we unite spirits.

The Library

Because the heart's staircase ascends the spine, spiraling up to your windowed brain,

    follow the clear soft-spoken voice leading you to the old oaken door

      ever so slightly cracked open, a warming hearth welcoming

        you to settle yourself in some wing-back chair,

          always aware of the hissing whisper

            asking *"Does God truly say?"*

Then peruse the walls surrounding you, the dust encroached within the corners,

    and observe the memories sheltered there on shelves less ordered than they should be.

      Explore the ideas trapped in covers, a forest of thoughts within one book

        where dragons lurk under the shadows, and engage the beast

          with wit and wisdom—captivate his very mind—

            and charm his words 'til he admits

"God does say so. I was wrong." his dispersing girth enabling light

    to shine on seeds too long hidden; the ancient treeman, crowned with thorns, smiling down

      while growth returns to the lily's fields. Please preserve this act, and then repeat

        in various settings treasured here: in brothels, bars, and the new high street;

          an ideal way to experience all

            gazing out from our glittering tower.

Polyphemus; Cyclops

No One remembers my name.
All ones remember my aesthetic.

Myopically, your memory recalls my sole eye,
that singular globe of perception, how I saw
my small isle, its caves, pastures, shorelines,
the domain I governed and cared for,
feeding and keeping the weakest of sheep
in lush, fragrant, valleys beside brethren
beneath the shadows of mountains, perilous,
aware of our Father in Heaven,
the Lord of the winds and the seas,
so confident his love for us children
would overwhelm our daily mistakes,
the uncouth demeanor, the desire for meat,

that I was surprised when your king's double-vision
gaveled down his penetrating weight,
condemning me brute, giant, monster,
although I'm really rather tiny and trusting,
unlike my neighbors, solitary,
accounting for all of my livestock,
longing for a female's taste,
and enjoying the occasional lyric,

and ready to defend my abode
against any invading pestilence,

amused by how I'm deemed "impolite"
while striving for diplomatic ends,

but now, in my blindness, I see your point.
Despite my meekness, I have killed,
been rendered a fool by your elixirs,
beseeched High Olympus for vengeance,
and complained when I received grace.

Thus, Poseidon has punished No One,
and decreed I should listen in this abyss
to whatever visions weird voices whisper
in the vacant cavern of my prism-skull,
nephalem blood and cherubim fire
exposing cloud-pillars and dawn-raising rays:
theophanies, prophecies, Tiresias, Deborah, Delphi,
unsummoned travelers who loom their tales
and permit me to boldly proclaim

I am Polyphemus, Cyclops,
abounding with legends and song.

"Deliver us from Evil"

For "the world is too much with us"—William Wordsworth

After warring in the field, exhausting,
I collapse on my bed in the hotel
as hypnotic clock-ticks start exposing
with the TV imperfections in my will,
molding character; the world's tempting words,
investment options, Italian dress-coats
at T-shirt prices, impressive cognacs,
captivating beauties who will gladly enact
intimate deeds to elicit a check,
and city-slick preachers hawking good health
and prosperity like watches set with cut-glass:
marrow for the coils Christ's heel crushed
though their venoms still need exorcizing.
Father, grant me your grace whom the Greeks named Athena,
her chaste, impregnable, mind in the helm of salvation,
the first child of creation in finest, pure, linens,
and direct her to dress me in Paul's metaphors
until I resemble an agile Spartan,
her gentle touches guiding my tongue like a spear,
and then on the day of my death's defeat,
let her hold my limp frame as a pieta
to contemplate its odyssey through time,
how every shrine turned foreign to its soul
when it rested in your love's true embrace.

Regeneration

Up, up, with ever encumbered steps I climb
from the sunken medieval citadel
foundationed inside the Louvre's basement;
up the limestone corridor I course
where titans stroll with leisure
beneath the stairway's exalted vaults;
up this temporal purgatory
I carry my body's weight to where

Victory lights on dove-like wings
above the globe's ascending masses.

Like a trireme's mast she stands
tall, uncrossed, her billowing feathers unfurled
as unseen gales clasp at her peplos
pulled taught against her nubile chest
and unswayed thighs
for she breaks herself through dense headwinds
to defend with rippling vestments
her hips' temple, that unplucked fig
concealed behind her exposed leg's bough.

Her faceless spirit moors inside my heart
to offer her my eyes
and leads me to her idol's feet
where, winded by vain advances,
I linger like a toddler
within his sister's shadow

until, impassioned by her blood
warmed below the ceiling's haloed window,
I voyage through the capillaries
of far-branching hallways

to where Venus, armless, a sacred matron,
dresses her loins in fine linens
and presents her milk-laden breasts
to pilgrims she has wooed

so they might discover somewhere else
Eros, her offspring,
descending on humble swallow-wings
to turn the marble frame of mortal Psyche
weightless in his embrace -
kissed.

The Writing on Our Walls

Like wax crayons crammed inside their cardboard box,
twenty-four colors labeled and in various states of abuse,
some broken, some dull, some reshaped after use
to recall how all were once perfectly molded,

a collection of people are pressed into an elevator
descending below London to the Underground
where we will spill out onto the subway's platforms
before travelling with others wherever the "Tube" takes us,

and amongst the overcoats, football kits, perfumes,
a young man in a well-weathered leather jacket
with headphones plugged into his pierced ears
bumps himself and his duffle bag into me,

revealing for a moment an assortment of rattle-cans.
Will he go, when steel doors lurch open, releasing psyches,
to a lorry, underpass, or canvas to spray
his beliefs into vibrant murals, comedic, grotesque,

even as I, so different, an American scholar,
trek to his kingdom's White Tower to study
crosses, curses, and confessions captives scratched into their cells,
aware that an axe would soon set them free?

—I now wonder a decade in the future
while penning these impressions with blue ink
in the periodical section of a Michiana public library:
perhaps a crayon selected in a cosmic Child's hand.

www.ingramcontent.com/pod-product-compliance
Lightning Source LLC
LaVergne TN
LVHW051706080426
835511LV00017B/2767